DAI

JOKES

ADVENT
CALENDER
2023

ABOUT MINDWORK BOOKS

Hey there, welcome to Mindwork Books! We're all about making learning and fun go hand in hand. Our books are designed to keep things simple, but interesting. No fancy jargon or complicated stuff - just good old-fashioned enjoyment.

What do we do? Well, we make coloring books, jokes, puzzles, and activity books that cater to everyone from little kids to grown-ups. Our mission is straightforward: we want learning to feel like a fun adventure. No drudgery, just excitement.

So, dive into our collection, and you'll find pages filled with colors that pop and puzzles that might make you scratch your head a bit. But that's the beauty of it – it's all about the joy of discovery.

If you've enjoyed our books, we'd love it if you could leave a review. Your thoughts keep us motivated and help us keep creating content that adds a dash of wonder to your day.

Thanks for choosing Mindwork Books. Let's keep it simple and have a blast while we learn!

Get ready for a sleigh ride of laughter as we unwrap the gift of dad humor. 'Tis the season to be merry and dad-joke-ready! 🎄

DAY 1

Santa's Workshop Wonders

Why did Santa's workshop apply for a loan?

Because it wanted to expand its business and "sleigh"

What do elves use to take notes in the workshop?

Elf-abet soup

Why did the toy train go to therapy?

It had too many issues with its "loco"-motion

Why did Santa take up gardening?

Because he wanted to hoe, hoe, hoe!

Why did Santa's helper see the doctor?

Because he had low "elf" esteem!

How does Santa keep his beard so neat?

He uses Claus-tarch!

What do you call Santa when he loses his pants?

Saint Knickerless!

Why did the elf apply for a job at the bakery?

Because he wanted to make gingerbread men!

Why did Santa go to music school?

To improve his wrapping skills!

DAY 2

Reindeer Antics

What do you call a reindeer with no eyes?

No-eye deer

Why did Rudolph the Red-Nosed Reindeer start a band?

Because he had the horns for it!

What do reindeer hang on their Christmas trees?

Hornaments

What do you get if you cross a reindeer and a detective?

Inspector Hoof!

What did one reindeer say to another before telling a joke?

"This will sleigh them!"

How do you know when Santa's reindeer are telling a joke?

You can hear their sleigh bells ringing!

What do you call a reindeer with a bad attitude?

Rude-olph!

Why did the reindeer start a podcast?

Because he had some great "deer" stories to share!

Why did the reindeer go to school?

To brush up on his "rein"-education!

DAY 3

Christmas Tree Troubles

Why was the Christmas tree so bad at sewing?

It kept dropping its needles!

What do you call a Christmas tree that solves crimes?

Sherlock Pines

Why did the Christmas tree break up with the ornament?

It couldn't handle the commitment

What did one Christmas tree say to the other?

"Stop needle-ing me!"

What do you call a Christmas tree that can dance?

Spruce Springsteen!

Why did the Christmas tree break up with the ornament?

It was tired of the same old decorations!

What do you get if you cross a Christmas tree with an iPad?

A pineapple!

What do you call a Christmas tree with no needles?

Spruce Willis!

Why did the Christmas tree apply for a job?

It wanted to be a tree-mendous success!

DAY 4

Candy Cane Capers

What's a snowman's favorite candy?

Frostbites!

Why did the candy cane go to school?

To get a little "mint"-elligence.

What do you call someone who steals energy drinks during the holidays?

A candy cane robber

Why did the candy cane go to the party alone?

It couldn't find its plus-one, peppermint!

Why did the candy cane refuse to fight?

It wanted to stay out of sticky situations!

How do you know if a candy cane is lying?

It'll be all twisted up!

What's a candy cane's favorite music?

Wrap music!

What did the candy cane say to the Christmas tree?

"You've got some serious bark!"

How do you catch a runaway candy cane?

Use a candy-cane trap, of course!

DAY 5

Snowman Shenanigans

What did one snowman say to the other?

"Do you smell carrots?"

Why did the snowman call his dog Frost?

Because Frost bites!

What do you get if you cross a snowman and a vampire?

Frostbite

How do you know if a snowman is smart?

It has snow-brainers!

What did the snowman say to the aggressive carrot?

"You better back off, I've got a corn cob and I'm not afraid to use it!"

What did one snowman say to the other?

"You're snow cool!"

What did the snowman say to the aggressive carrot?

"Get out of my face, I'm not ready to nose you!"

What do you call a snowman with a sense of humor?

Frosty the Joke Man!

Why did the snowman call his friend on a frosty day?

He wanted to have a "cool" conversation!

DAY 6

Elves on Break

What do you call an elf who sings?

A wrapper!

Why did the elf go to therapy?

He had low elf-esteem

How do elves greet each other?

"Small world, isn't it?"

Why did the elf become a detective?

He was great at "wrapping" up cases!

How do elves greet each other during the holidays?
"Buddy, it's been a while!"

Why did the elf bring a thermos to the workshop?
He wanted to stay "hot" on the job!

Why did the elf refuse to play hide and seek?

Because good luck hiding when you jingle with every step!

Why did the elf bring a pencil to the cookie factory?
To use it as a "whisk"!

How do elves keep their hair in place?
With "elf-gel"!

DAY 7

Gingerbread House Humor

Why did the gingerbread man go to the doctor?

He was feeling crumby.

What do you call a gingerbread house on a diet?

A lean-to.

How do you catch a gingerbread man?

Use ginger snaps!

What did the gingerbread man use to fix his car?

Ginger-ale!

How do gingerbread houses keep their secrets?

They lock them in the ginger-vault!

What do you call a gingerbread man with one leg bitten off?

Limp Bizkit!

What did the gingerbread man say to his icing?

"You make everything a little sweeter!"

Why did the gingerbread man apply for a loan?

He needed a little extra dough for his mortgage!

How do you know if a gingerbread house is haunted?

You hear ginger-boo sounds!

DAY 8

Mistletoe Mishaps

What did one mistletoe say to another?

"Hang in there!"

Why did the Christmas tree break up with the mistletoe?

It wasn't ready to settle down and wanted to remain a free branchelor.

What did the mistletoe say to the ceiling?

"I've got you covered!"

What did the mistletoe write in its diary?

"Another day of being overlooked, yet so close to the action!"

What did one mistletoe say to the other during a disagreement?

"Let's kiss and makeup!"

Why did the tomato blush under the mistletoe?

It saw the salad dressing!

What do you call a person who steals mistletoe?

A kiss-napper!

How did the mistletoe respond to criticism?

It brushed it off, saying, "I'm just here for the smooches!"

What did one mistletoe say to the other?

"Hang around, I'm not ready to leaf yet!"

DAY 9

Stocking Stuffer Surprises

What do you call a snowman
with a six-pack?

An abdominal snowman.

Why did the stocking go to
therapy?

It had too many issues with its
inseam.

How does Santa keep his pants
up?

With an elf belt.

Why did the stocking get promoted?

It had a great sense of "stock" market trends!

What did the stocking say to the gift?

"You really know how to sock it to me!"

How does a stocking apologize?

It says, "I really toe-tally messed up!"

What do you call a stocking that sings?

A wrap star!

Why did the stocking refuse to go bungee jumping?

It was afraid of getting hung up!

What's a stocking's favorite type of movie?

Anything with a good "twist" ending!

DAY 10

Sleigh Ride
Ridiculousness

What did the gingerbread man say as he rode Santa's sleigh?

"You better dasher away!"

Why was the snowman looking through the carrots?

He was picking his nose.

What do you call a snowman with a sunburn?

A puddle.

What's Santa's favorite type of ride?

A sleigh ride, of course—it's "sleighin'"!

What do you call a snowman on Santa's sleigh?

A snow-boarder!

Why did Santa take his sleigh to the auto shop?

It had a bad case of "snow-motion"!

How do you know if Santa is good at music?

He always sleighs the guitar!

Why did the elf bring a camera on the sleigh?

He wanted to capture the "sleighfie" moments!

Why did Santa's reindeer start a band?

Because they had the drumsticks!

DAY 11

North Pole
Nonsense

What do you get when you cross a snowman and a vampire at the North Pole?

Frostbite!

Why did the North Pole apply for a bank loan?

To get its ig-loans in order.

What do you call a polar bear in the desert?

Lost.

Why did the penguin start a business at the North Pole?

He wanted to break the ice in the market!

What's Santa's favorite snack at the North Pole?

Ice Krispies!

How do you make a tissue dance at the North Pole?

You put a little "boogie" in it!

What did Santa say to the smoker at the North Pole?

Please don't "puffin" here!

Why did the reindeer bring a GPS to the North Pole?

They wanted to navigate the "ho-ho-ho"-rizon!

How do you send a letter to Santa from the North Pole?

Use the "polar" express!

DAY 12

Holiday Shopping Hilarity

Why did the ornament go to therapy?

It couldn't find its center.

Why did the Christmas shopper bring a ladder to the store?

Because they heard the prices were through the roof!

How do you know if Santa is good at karate while shopping?

He has a black belt in gift-wrapping!

What did the snowman say to the holiday sale?

"I'm flaking out over these prices!"

Why did the Christmas lights go to therapy after holiday shopping?

They felt a bit tangled up!

Why did the ornament go to the mall?

It wanted to hang out with its friends!

What did the gift say to the wrapping paper?

"You really know how to wrap things up!"

What do you call a snowman who does all his shopping online?

Frosty the Click-Man!

How do you know if Santa is good at shopping?

He always sleighs the deals!

DAY 13

Christmas Carol Comedy

What carol is heard in the desert?

"Camel Ye Faithful."

Why was the snowman a great singer?

He had the coolest voice.

What's a snowman's favorite cereal?

Frosted Flakes.

Why did Frosty go to the party solo?

He couldn't find his snow-date!

What do you get if you cross Frosty with a detective?

Sherlock Flakes!

Why did Frosty become a detective?

He was good at finding "cold" cases!

What do snowmen call their offspring?

Chill-dren!

What's Frosty's favorite type of dance?

The snowball!

Why did Frosty go to school?

To improve his "cool"-culus!

DAY 14

Festive Feast Funnies

Why did the cranberry turn red?

Because it saw the turkey dressing.

What do you get if you eat Christmas decorations?

Tinselitis.

What do you call a snowman with a credit card?

Frosty the Snowspender!

What did the pumpkin pie say to the pecan pie?

"You're one tough nut to crack!"

Why did the turkey sit in the corner of the table?

Because it was stuffed!

Why did the cranberry turn to the blueberry?

It was feeling a bit jammed!

What did the mashed potatoes say to the gravy?

"You're my butter half!"

Why did the turkey sit on the dinner table?

To gobble up all the attention!

Why did the turkey join the band?

Because it had the drumsticks!

DAY 15

Winter Weather Woes

What do snowmen like to do on the weekend?

Chill out.

How do snowmen get around?

By riding an "icicle."

What do you call Santa when he takes a break from delivering presents?

Santa Pause!

What did the snowflake say to the wind?

"Stop blowing me around!"

Why did the winter hat go to the doctor?
It had a bad case of the "cold sweats"!

Why did the snowman bring a carrot to the winter party?

In case he got hungry for a "snack-arrot"!

Why did the snowman go to therapy?

He had too many "melt"-downs!

Why did the snowman bring a bucket to the winter storm?
In case he had to "chill" out!

What did the winter hat say to the scarf?

"You really suit me!"

DAY 16

Fruitcake Funniness

Why did the fruitcake go to therapy?

It had too many layers of issues.

What did the fruitcake say to the Christmas cookies?

"You're really in a jam!"

How does a fruitcake answer the phone?

"Fruitcake speaking!"

Why did the fruitcake apply for a job in a bakery?

It kneaded a change!

How did the fruitcake become the class clown?

It had a talent for "rind"-iculous jokes!

What do you get if you cross a fruitcake and a pineapple?

A tropical disaster!

How does a fruitcake answer the phone?

"Mellow?"

Why did the fruitcake become a detective?

It wanted to "uncover" the mysteries of the holiday season!

How do you make a fruitcake laugh?

Tell it a "berry" good joke!

DAY 17

New Year's
Resolutions
Reckoning

Why did the snowman break up with the calendar?

He thought their days were numbered.

What's Santa's New Year's resolution?

To be more Claus-trophobic!

Why did the gingerbread man resolve to be more positive?

He wanted to be a little sweeter.

What did the vegetable say to the
New Year's resolution?

"Lettuce stick to our goals!"

What's the resolution of a pun
enthusiast?

To make everyone laugh—no
"punning" intended!

What do you call a resolution
that involves laughter?

A "giggle"-ution!

What did the clock say to the calendar on New Year's Eve?

"See you next year!"

Why did the resolution go to the gym?

It wanted to get into better "shape"!

What's a procrastinator's New Year's resolution?

To start working on resolutions... next year!

DAY 18

Jingle Bell Jests

What did one bell say to the other?

"You ring my chimes!"

Why did the Christmas bell go to school?

To get a little "ring"-elligence.

How do snowmen greet each other?

Ice to meet you!

What do you call Santa's little helpers?

Subordinate clauses!

How does Santa take pictures?

With his North Pole-aroid!

Why did the Christmas ornament go to school?

It wanted to be a little "brighter"!

What do you call Santa when he takes a vacation?

Krisp Kring-leisure!

How does Santa keep track of all the fireplaces he's visited?

He keeps a log!

Why was the music teacher so good at playing Jingle Bells?

Because she had perfect "sleigh"!

DAY 19

Holiday Movie Mayhem

Why did Frosty the Snowman want a divorce?

His wife was a total flake.

What's Santa's favorite action movie?

Sleigh Hard.

Why was the Christmas tree so bad at playing cards?

It was always dealing.

Why did the Christmas lights go to the movie theater?

They wanted to see a "sparkling" performance!

Why did the Christmas present refuse to watch scary movies?

It was afraid it might get "unwrapped"!

What did the Christmas stocking say after watching a movie?

"That was a real stocking stuffer of a film!"

What did the snowman say after watching a romantic holiday movie?

"I'm feeling a little melty!"

What did the Christmas tree say after watching a movie?

"I'm pining for a sequel!"

What's a snowman's favorite movie genre?

Chillers!

DAY 20

Ugly Sweater Laughs

Why did the sweater break up with the scarf?

It felt a little too wrapped up in the relationship.

What's a snowman's favorite type of clothing?

An "icicle" dress.

Why did the Christmas sweater go to therapy?

It had too many unraveling issues.

What's an ugly sweater's favorite dance move?

The "woolly" mambo!

Why did the ugly sweater start a band?

It wanted to "knit" some tunes together!

What did the ugly sweater say to the warm fireplace?

"I'm feeling a little hot under the collar!"

How did the ugly sweater win the talent show?

It had everyone in stitches!

What do you call a group of ugly sweaters?

A knit-wit convention!

How do you know if a sweater is telling a joke?

It'll have you in stitches!

DAY 21

Yuletide Yoga

What do you call Santa when he takes a break?

Krisp Kingle.

Why did Santa start doing yoga?

To improve his "present"-ation.

How does Santa stay in shape during the off-season?

Claus and effect.

How does Santa relax after a long night of delivering presents?

He practices "sleigh"-vasana!

What did the Christmas stocking say during yoga?

"I'm stocking up on inner peace!"

How do snowmen practice mindfulness?

They take deep "frosty"-breaths!

What do you call a reindeer who practices yoga?

A "Zen"-deer!

What's Santa's favorite yoga pose?

The sleigh-asana!

How do you greet someone during yuletide yoga?

"Namaste-lly jolly!"

DAY 22

Christmas Card Capers

Why did the Christmas card apply for a job?

It wanted to get into the "envelope"-ment industry.

What did one Christmas card say to the other?

"Have an un-fur-gettable holiday!"

How do snowmen send their love letters?

With frost-class postage.

What do you call a Christmas card that tells jokes?

A "laughing stock"!

Why did the Christmas card start a band?

It had great notes!

Why did the Christmas card bring a pencil to the party?

It wanted to draw some attention!

How does a Christmas card stay fit?

It does a lot of "card"-io exercises!

Why did the Christmas card break up with the envelope?

It felt a bit "enclosed" in the relationship!

How does a Christmas card apologize?

It says, "I didn't mean to be so 'paparazzi'!"

DAY 23

Eggnog Extravaganza

Why did the eggnog go to therapy?

It had too many issues with its "eggs"-istential crisis.

What do you call eggnog that's been left out too long?

Spoiled nog.

Why did the eggnog break up with the whipped cream?

It couldn't handle the fluff.

How does eggnog relax?

It takes a "chill" pill!

Why did the eggnog bring a spoon to the party?

In case things got a little "stir-crazy"!

Why did the eggnog go to the gym?

It wanted to be "eggs"-tra fit for the holiday season!

What did the gingerbread man say to the eggnog?

"You're 'nog'-thing without me!"

Why did the eggnog apply for a job?

It wanted to make some "holiday dough"!

What did the whipped cream say to the eggnog?

"You're my favorite topping!"

DAY 24

Fireplace Funnies

Why did the fire refuse to play cards?

It was afraid of getting burned.

What did one log say to the other in the fireplace?

"You really know how to ignite my passion."

How does Santa keep warm in the workshop?

He stands close to the elf-ment.

Why did the chimney break up
with the fireplace?

It needed some space!

What did the fireplace say to the
candles during a power outage?

"Let's keep the flame alive!"

Why did the fireplace get a
promotion?

It was great at keeping things
"heated"!

How does a fireplace celebrate its birthday?

With a "blazing" cake!

Why did the firewood go to school?

It wanted to be a "bright" student!

Why did the fireplace break up with the woodpile?

It wanted a relationship that wasn't so one-sided!

DAY 25

Christmas

What did the Christmas tree say to the ornament?

"Quit hanging around, you're really starting to weigh me down!"

Why did Santa bring a ladder to the Christmas party?

He heard the drinks were on the house!

Why did Santa bring a broom to the Christmas party?

He wanted to sweep everyone off their feet!

Why did Rudolph refuse to play reindeer games?

He was "dashing" through the snow!

Why did the Christmas tree go to the barber?

It needed a trim!

Why did the ornament go to therapy?

It had too many "hang-ups"!

What's Santa's favorite type of candy on Christmas Day?

Jolly ranchers!

What do snowmen eat for lunch on Christmas Day?

Icebergers!

Why did the Christmas cat sit on the computer?

It wanted to keep an eye on the mouse!

Merry Christmas!

Printed in Great Britain
by Amazon

33341689R00059